For
Fred and Martha Mahan

John Paul II

(a short biography)

• • •

KERRY WALTERS

Franciscan
MEDIA
Cincinnati, Ohio

Cover and book design by Mark Sullivan
Cover image © 1987 Catholic News Service | Joe Rinkus, Jr.

LIBRARY OF CONGRESS CATALOGING-IN-PUBLICATION DATA
Walters, Kerry S.
John Paul II : a short biography / Kerry Walters.
        .   pages cm
Includes bibliographical references and index.
ISBN 978-1-61636-749-7 (alk. paper)
1. John Paul II, Pope, 1920-2005. 2. Popes—Biography. I. Title.
BX1378.5.W355 2013
282.092—dc23
[B]
                                        2013037600

ISBN 978-1-61636-749-7

Published by Franciscan Media
28 W. Liberty St.
Cincinnati, OH 45202
www.FranciscanMedia.org

Printed in the United States of America.
Printed on acid-free paper.
14 15 16 17 18   5 4 3 2 1

Contents

Introduction: *A Saint for Our Time, vii*

. . .

Chapter One: *Early Trials and Graces, 1*

Chapter Two: *Seminarian and Priest, 6*

Chapter Three: *Defender of Church and Faith, 11*

Chapter Four: *Peter's Successor, 16*

Chapter Five: *Redemptive Suffering, 21*

Chapter Six: *At Odds with the World, 26*

Chapter Seven: *Blessed Are the Peacemakers, 31*

Chapter Eight: *Duc in altum!, 36*

Chapter Nine: *Preaching from the Cross, 41*

. . .

Conclusion: *Legacy, 46*

Notes, *48*

Bibliography, *52*

Introduction

A Saint for Our Time

"Transcendent holiness, which is in a sense 'outside the World,' becomes in Christ a holiness which is 'in the world.'"[1]

—John Paul II, *Gift and Mystery*

John Paul II was one of the most influential men of our time. The spiritual leader of over a billion Christians, he was a recognized world leader as well.

His moral authority helped break the grip of communism on his native Poland and jump-start the velvet revolutions that brought down the Soviet Union in 1989. He tirelessly urged nations to find nonviolent alternatives to war, reduce poverty and discrimination, and eliminate abortion, euthanasia, and capital punishment. He reached out to tens of thousands of young people in annual worldwide rallies, championed the natural environment before doing so became fashionable, encouraged ecumenical collaboration and interfaith dialogue, and despite his opposition to ordaining women, defended gender equality in the workplace.

John Paul wrote poems and plays, several books on philosophy and theology, fourteen encyclicals, thirty-six apostolic letters, and thousands of pages of magisterial documents. He traveled around the globe several times over to deliver nearly four thousand sermons and speeches to millions of people, Christian and non-Christian alike. Known as a firm ruler of the Church, he also humbly begged forgiveness for past crimes and misdemeanors committed by churchmen. And he showed the world how to die with patience, grace, and faith. Within hours of his passing, people were calling him "John Paul the Great" and shouting "*Santo subito!*"—"Sainthood now!"

Serving as pope doesn't by itself warrant sainthood. Fewer than a third of the pontiffs have been canonized. Nor is performing great deeds in the world, however admirable they may be, a sufficient qualification. Still less is mere celebrity.

Perfection isn't a necessary condition for sainthood either. Such purity is reserved for God alone, and we risk transforming genuine saints into saccharine caricatures if we try to bestow it on them. Saints throughout the history of Christianity have wrestled with shortcomings, doubts, weaknesses, confusions, and occasionally outright sinfulness. St. John Paul is no exception in this regard. Critics as well as many of his admirers have pointed out that his pontificate was a bit too magisterial and his response to the scandal of sex abuse in the Church a bit too slow. He was a man of incredible faith and uncommon decency. But he was, after all, human, as all saints are.

What makes a saint—what makes John Paul a saint—is not ecclesial and worldly titles or unquestionable moral and spiritual purity, but a yearningly tenacious cleaving to the Creator, a heartfelt resolution to embrace in word and deed our own God-likeness despite the realization that we'll often fall short, and a willingness to spend ourselves in loving service to God and one another. John Paul himself described sainthood in terms of holiness. "Holiness," he wrote, "is to raise one's eyes to the summits. It is intimacy with God the Father who is in Heaven. In this intimacy, each one of us is aware of our nature, with all its limitations and difficulties."[2]

Reading the lives of holy men and women can inspire us to strive for holiness in our own limited and difficult lives. But sometimes they can seem too historically remote to serve as fruitful role models for us. Not so with John Paul II. He was a man of our time. Now he's a saint for our time.

chapter one

Early Trials and Graces

"In our trials we may feel alone, but God's grace, the grace
of a victorious faith, will never abandon us."[3]
—John Paul II, *Rise, Let Us Be On Our Way*

It would be understandable if the boy Karol Józef Wojtyła had
grown into a bitter man haunted by unhappy memories. As he once
said, he had lost everyone he loved by the time he was twenty. That
he didn't grow bitter is a testament to the moments of grace that
punctuated the sorrow of his early years. The trials that burdened
him and the graces that sustained him were the first steps in the
future pope's apprenticeship in sainthood.

Affectionately called Lolek by his parents, Karol Wojtyła was born
in the leap year of 1920. His birthplace, Wadowice, was a Polish
town located about fifty kilometers from Kraków. Although pro-
vincial, Wadowice boasted three libraries, several private schools,
a cinema, and a theater. It was also intensely Catholic in the sometimes dark and brooding style of the early twentieth-century Polish
Church.

Lolek's only living sibling, his elder brother Edmund, left home to study medicine when Lolek was still a toddler. Lolek adored Edmund but saw him only when he returned home during university holidays. So for all practical purposes, the boy was raised as an only child, and primarily by his father, who was also named Karol.

Lolek's mother, Emilia, had been sickly and frequently bedridden for as long as Lolek could remember. As her health worsened, Karol Sr. took on more and more domestic responsibility, finally retiring on a meager pension in 1927 to care full-time for her and their son. In the weeks before she finally died in 1929, just a month shy of Lolek's ninth birthday, Emilia sank into a black, uncommunicative depression that further distanced her from her grieving younger son.

His mother's death left Lolek with a crushing sense of abandonment that marked him, as one of his teachers observed, with the "shadow of an early sorrow."[4] Nine years afterward, Lolek tried to express the intensity of his desolation in a heartbreaking poem, "Mother, my lifeless love."

> Over this your white grave
> the flowers of life in white—
> so many years without you—
> how many have passed out of sight?[5]

Two and a half years later, still grieving for his mother, Lolek's world collapsed again. His beloved Edmund, who had received his medical degree in 1930, caught scarlet fever from a patient and died in Kraków. Pope John Paul once said that he felt his brother's loss even more intensely than his mother's. Throughout his entire pontificate, he kept a cherished relic, Edmund's old stethoscope, in his Vatican apartment.

Father and son were devastated by this latest death in the family, and both turned to God in their sorrow. Already pious, they now embraced an almost monastic devotional discipline. Karol Sr. often spent the entire night in prayer. For his part, Lolek served at one and sometimes two or three Masses every day, prayed before and after school, and often sat in silent adoration in front of the Blessed Sacrament. It was during this period of intense mourning and equally intense prayer that Lolek became interested in the writings of St. John of the Cross, especially the Spanish mystic's reflections on the spiritual despair he called the dark night of the soul.

Part of Lolek's attraction to John of the Cross was the beauty of his poetry and prose. As John Paul recalled years later, it was around this time that he became "completely absorbed by a passion for literature, especially dramatic literature, and for the theater."[6] His reading led him to try his hand at writing plays and poetry, and he discovered a talent for acting and directing as well. Literature and religion helped Lolek cope with his sorrow by revealing to him a deep beauty and purposiveness to existence.

His devotion to God and passion for literature deepened after he and his father moved to Kraków in the late summer of 1938 so that he could matriculate at Jagiellonian University, his brother's alma mater. Now eighteen, Karol threw himself into the study of Polish literature and language, continued to write verse—he would cease only when elected pope forty years later—and became an active member of the Rhapsodic Theater, an acting troupe that focused on the spoken word rather than costumes and set.

There he also met one of the most remarkable men of his day, the reclusive mystic Jan Tyranowski, who invited him to join the Living Rosary, a band of young men dedicated to living the fifteen mysteries in their daily lives. John Paul once described Tyranowksi as "one of those unknown saints, hidden like a marvelous light at the bottom of life, at a depth where night usually reigns."[7]

Karol had just begun his second year of university studies when the Nazis invaded Poland. The first German bombs rained on Kraków in September 1939; within a week, the city fell. Determined to obliterate "inferior" Slavic culture, the Nazi occupiers closed down universities and schools and arrested their faculties. Because Polish culture and Catholicism were so closely intertwined, the Nazis also forbade the celebration of religious holidays; shipped priests, nuns, and monks by the hundreds to concentration camps; and outlawed religious fraternities and seminaries.

As winter set in, food and supplies in the occupied city became scarce. "Now life is waiting in line for bread, scavenging for sugar, and dreaming of coal and books,"[8] Karol wrote to a friend. To make ends meet, and to keep from being sent to work in a German munitions factory, he took a job at a local quarry, where he was assigned for the first few months to laying railroad tracks and breaking stone with a pickax.

The heavy labor, often in bitterly cold weather, was hard on Karol. But he was sustained by his participation in the Living Rosary—which, if discovered by the Nazis, would have brought harsh retribution—and the Rhapsodic Theater. Both activities not only refreshed his soul—they were also ways of resisting the occupiers, yet another grace.

Then, in the third winter of the occupation, the third and greatest loss of his young life struck. Returning from work to the basement apartment he shared with his father, he discovered that Karol Sr., who had been ailing since December, had died. Karol was inconsolable, first with regret—"I wasn't there when my mother died," he lamented, "I wasn't there when my brother died, I wasn't there when my father died"[9]—and then with a crushing sense of forlornness. As he later confided to an acquaintance, "I never felt so alone."[10]

chapter two

Seminarian and Priest

"The one about to receive Holy Orders prostrates himself completely and rests his forehead on the church floor, indicating in this way his complete willingness to undertake the ministry being entrusted to him."[11]

—John Paul II, *Gift and Mystery*

Although Karol didn't realize it until a few months after his father's death, his friends and acquaintances had long sensed he had a vocation to the priesthood. Even before the blow of losing loved ones deepened his interior life, he was noted for his piety—not the shallow, showy kind, but one that bespoke regular and intense prayer, reflection, and unshakable faith.

After being assigned less physically taxing work in a factory, Karol had more time and energy to read, pray, and think about where God wanted him to go. In August 1942, he notified Adam Sapieha, the Prince Archbishop of Kraków, that he wanted to be a priest.

Sapieha, an impressively lineaged patrician who refused to flee the Nazi invasion, collaborated with the Polish resistance movement, issued false baptismal documents to Kraków's Jews to protect them from roundups, and offered shelter in his palace to refugees fleeing the Gestapo. He accepted Karol as an underground seminarian, cautioning him to keep his job so as not to draw attention to himself. Classes for Karol and his nine fellow students were taught in private homes, churches, and even outdoors. Caution was essential: Five of Sapieha's underground seminarians were discovered and shot.

John Paul always maintained that he'd attended two earlier seminaries before Sapieha's. In one, his father had taught him austerity, discipline, and humble devotion. In the other, the quarry workers had shown him the value of physical labor and the dignity of those who perform it. As pope, he would explore these themes in his third papal encyclical, the 1981 *Laborem Exercens*.

In the underground seminary, Karol continued to read John of the Cross, and found himself increasingly attracted to the contemplative life. Nearly killed in the winter of 1944 by a German military lorry, he convalesced for three weeks in a hospital room overlooking a Carmelite monastery. Later describing the experience as a "spiritual retreat sent from God,"[12] he saw it as a sign that he should become a Carmelite.

But Archbishop Sapieha had other plans. Postwar Poland was badly in need of parish priests. So after ordaining Karol in 1946, he sent him to Rome for further study, where the young priest dove even deeper into the writings of John of the Cross. He originally had turned to the Spanish Carmelite as a source of comfort for his grief over his brother's death. But he came to see the saint's doctrine of the dark night of the soul as an important message to a world shattered by war and genocide. John's insight, Pope John Paul wrote in the apostolic letter Master in the Faith, was that "even the experience of [God's] absence can communicate faith, love, and hope to one who humbly and meekly opens himself to God."[13]

When Karol returned from Rome, Sapieha sent him first to a backwater village so remote that it lacked running water and electricity, and then, a few months later, to a thriving parish in the heart of Kraków frequented by students from nearby Jagiellonian University. In the first assignment, Karol made his parish rounds in a horse cart and sometimes pitched in to help villagers dig ditches or harvest crops. In the second, he traveled by car or bicycle, taught ethics at the university, and wrote scholarly essays. But three things were the same in both places.

First and foremost, Father Karol was utterly and tirelessly devoted to his priestly calling. While he acknowledged that the death of his father and the horror of a world at war had been factors in his turning to the Church, he also knew that he'd been called by the Holy Spirit to tend souls and that his responsibility as a priest was therefore incalculable. He never wanted to take his calling for granted, he once told a fellow seminarian, much less to tarnish "apostolic values" by neglecting his own relationship with God. He was convinced that in the absence of an authentic prayer life, "a priest will imperceptibly turn into an office clerk."[14] So for his own sake, not to mention his parishioners', the priest should always remember that he is a "steward of the mysteries of God," and that there is no "greater fulfillment of [his] humanity than to be able to re-present every day *in persona Christi* the redemptive sacrifice."[15]

Second, Karol brought to both his parishes a spirit of Franciscan-like poverty that amused some and shocked others but won the respect of most. Although always clean, his cassocks were old, frayed around the edges and shiny at the knees from much prayer. He arrived at his two assignments with only a single ragged suitcase and an armload of books. Whenever parishioners gave him a new sweater or jacket, he always passed it on to someone else in need.

Finally, Father Karol displayed a real gift for ministering to young people. He knew how to relate to them on their own terms, earn their respect and affection, and make the truths of Christianity come alive for them. They responded enthusiastically, calling him "*Wujek*" ("Uncle") as a token of their trust. In both of his parishes, *Wujek* Karol organized regular hikes and camping holidays in which he and a dozen or so young people retreated into the mountains and forests of Poland. Their day's activities were prefaced by a Mass using an altar of piled stones or upturned canoe, and afterward, while exploring the terrain or sitting before a campfire, Karol made a point of listening to and counseling his young wards. The advice he gave them on marriage, sexuality, and relationships would later find its way into a couple of books: *Love and Responsibility,* a treatise on ethics, and *The Jeweler's Shop,* a play.

By 1958, Karol Wojtyła's priestly ministry seemed settled. But then he received an invitation—a summons, really—to present himself at the Warsaw palace of Cardinal Stefan Wyszyński, Primate of Poland.

chapter three

Defender of Church and Faith

> "St. Stanisław…dared to tell the king himself that he was
> bound to respect the law of God."[16]
> —Cardinal Karol Wojtyła, Pastoral Letter, May 8, 1977

There was something about Father Karol that irritated Primate Wyszyński right from the start. Temperamentally, the two men couldn't have been more different. Karol was a scholar who related easily to workers and students. The cardinal was distrustful of intellectuals and had a reputation for aloof haughtiness.

When Archbishop Adam Sapieha died in 1951, his successor took Karol under his wing. By 1958, he was so impressed by the young priest that he asked the Vatican to name Karol his auxiliary bishop. But he bypassed Wyszyński's office, and the first the primate heard of it was when he received a letter from Pius XII ordering him to approve the appointment. So Wyszyński was in a cold rage when he called Karol to his office to tell him he was to be a bishop. It took the primate years to overcome his resentment.

Wojtyła was consecrated bishop on September 28, 1958. One month to the day later, the seventy-seven-year-old patriarch of

Venice, Angelo Roncalli, was elected pope, taking the name John XXIII. Because of his advanced age, nobody expected much from him. But three months after his election, the new John called for an ecumenical council that brought some two thousand bishops to Rome to breathe the spirit of *aggiornamento* into the Church. Wojtyła was one of them. As was his wont when deeply moved, he expressed his excitement in verse:

> Poor and naked, we will be transparent as glass
> that both cuts and reflects.
> Lashed by conscience, this vast temple its setting,
> The split world must grow whole.[17]

As befit a newly consecrated bishop, Wojtyła kept a low profile in the first of the Council's session. But by the fourth and final one in 1965, he had become the spokesman for the Polish delegation. Wojtyła's own views on the council demonstrate that it is too simplistic to casually label him conservative or liberal. He agreed with the reformers who believed that the Roman Curia possessed too much authority and the bishops too little. So he wholeheartedly embraced the council's spirit of power-sharing.

But he vigorously—and unsuccessfully, as it turned out—resisted *Gaudium et Spes*'s proclamation that because the Church lives and works within world history, it should be willing to learn from other religious faiths and from secular society. Wojtyła and the rest of the Polish delegation took the more traditional position that the Church was a perfect and transcendent institution founded by and mystically united with Christ, and therefore the only repository of truth.

While defending the transcendent nature of the Church before the council, Wojtyła was also busy defending the faith back in his native land. At the end of World War II, Poland had become an unwilling satellite of the Soviet Union and had endured a series of Stalinist campaigns to transform it into a collectivist state. In their drive to please their Kremlin masters, Poland's communist leaders inaugurated economic programs that left the nation virtually bankrupt. They also steadily persecuted the Church as a reactionary and superstitious institution.

Back in the days of Nazi occupation, young Karol thought that prayer was the best form of resistance to political repression. During the communist years, he still put prayer first and foremost. But as a leader of the Church, Bishop Wojtyła concluded that it was his responsibility to defend the faith by word and deed as well. In Poland, this meant taking a stand for basic human rights such as religious freedom.

The Church, Wojtyła believed, must provide an alternative to the spiritual emptiness of communism. Poland's leaders triumphantly announced the death of God as often as they could. But they never grasped the self-defeating nihilism of their message, because if God *is* dead, then all of human existence, including class struggle, becomes meaningless.

Wojtyła's way of responding to state atheism was steady and firm rather than flamboyant. In 1962, for example, he quietly but persistently protested the state's seizure of a seminary building, and succeeded in getting the authorities to back down. He also began a decade-long campaign for the construction of a church in Nowa Huta, the communist regime's model socialist community on the outskirts of Kraków.

The authorities envisioned Nowa Huta as utterly secular. But to shut Wojtyła up, they gave him a patch of land on which to construct his church while holding up the actual building permits year after year. Every Christmas, Wojtyła embarrassed the government by celebrating midnight Mass on the empty lot. The authorities finally backed down, and the church was built. To show its approval of Wojtyła's efforts, the Vatican sent a stone from the Emperor Constantine's first basilica to include in the church's foundation.

The Nowa Huta campaign was part of Wojtyła's larger one to keep the Church alive in Poland. He submitted dozens of requests each year for new seminaries and churches, swiftly condemned every act of religious discrimination, and resisted the state's efforts to abolish religious education. He collaborated with *Odrodzenie* ("Rebirth") an underground organization whose goal was to train lay Catholics for leadership. In hundreds of sermons, speeches, newspaper articles, and essays, he proclaimed the truth of Christianity and the necessity of human freedom. He regularly appealed to the example of the eleventh-century St. Stanisław, martyred for defying the tyrants of his day.

Truth, Wojtyła insisted, is the best weapon against "an authority based on police truncheons."[18] And because truth is one, undivided and whole, Christ's message of liberation is material as well as spiritual, pertaining to the body politic as well as to the individual soul. It was a message that Poland's communist leaders weren't anxious for the people to hear. But Wojtyla's growing authority as a leader of the Church made it difficult to silence him.

Peter's Successor

"Brothers and sisters, don't be afraid to welcome Christ
and to accept his power."[19]

—John Paul II, Inaugural Mass Homily

In December 1963, Wojtyła was named Archbishop of Kraków. In
what must have struck him as a sad irony, his appointment was
readily accepted by the Poland's communist leaders, who thought
him too bookish to cause any trouble, but resisted by Primate
Wyszyński, who still disliked him.

Wojtyła's participation in Vatican II as well as his determined ministry in Poland soon brought him to the attention of Paul IV, who
succeeded John XXIII in the summer of 1963. Paul made Wojtyła
a cardinal in 1967—to Wyszyński's dismay—and enlisted his aid
in writing the controversial encyclical on birth control, *Humanae
Vitae*. In 1969, Cardinal Wojtyła published a treatise on philo-
sophical anthropology entitled *Person and Act*. The book made his
reputation as a philosopher, but its argument was so dense that
seminarians soon wisecracked that the pain of slogging through it
was as good as a get-out-of-purgatory-free card.

Popes do not name their successors, but they frequently offer hints at who they hope will follow them. Paul VI signaled his wishes in 1976 by inviting Wojtyła to give the Vatican Lenten retreat. Despite this clear mark of favor, the 450-year-old tradition of electing only Italian popes was too strong to break when Paul died the following year. Albino Luciano, the gentle patriarch of Venice, succeeded to the throne and took the name John Paul. Shortly afterward, he told the Vatican secretary of state that Cardinal Wojtyła should have been the enclave's choice. Only a few weeks later, John Paul died unexpectedly. This time, the college of cardinals *did* choose Wojtyła, who took the name John Paul II. He was only fifty-eight, in vigorous health, and unboundedly energetic.

At his inaugural mass, John Paul did two things that signaled the direction of his pontificate. When an aged Wyszyński knelt before him to kiss his papal ring as a sign of obedience, the pope knelt in turn before the aged primate and embraced him, publicly ending their feud. Later, in his homily, John Paul called on all Christians everywhere to serve Christ by fearlessly serving their fellow humans. In both deed and word, the new pope announced to the world that he intended to seek reconciliation, champion human rights, and speak for the "Church of Silence" behind the Iron Curtain.

As a Christian and priest, nothing was more important to Karol Wojtyła than his devotion to God. But as John Paul II, he knew he was also called to defy the Soviet system. The Church, as he would write in *Redemptor Hominis,* the encyclical he published only five months after his election, was called to be priest, prophet, and servant-king to the world, and this meant speaking truth to repressive power.

But to do this, John Paul had to venture beyond the Vatican. In January 1979 he made the first of what would be scores of pastoral journeys, flying to Puebla, Mexico, to attend a conference of Latin American bishops. While there, John Paul clarified his position on liberation theology, an amalgamation of Catholic social teaching and Marxist analysis that responded to brutally oppressive right-wing regimes in countries like Nicaragua and El Salvador.

The pope vigorously condemned what he saw as liberation theology's efforts to politicize Jesus. Church doctrine, he said, already opposed "all forms of domination, slavery, and discrimination," and had "no need to resort to systems and ideologies" such as Marxism.[20] Leftists criticized John Paul for what they saw as his conflation of Eastern-bloc Stalinism and Latin American liberation theology. Conservatives seized on his remarks to self-servingly justify the preservation of oppressive status quos. For his part, the pope continued to insist that the Gospel of Christ was sufficient for both spiritual and political liberation. "It is not just, it is not human, it is not Christian, to continue with certain situations that are clearly unjust."[21]

Five months later, John Paul traveled to his beloved Poland with the same message. For nine days he journeyed throughout the country speaking to an estimated ten million Poles who everywhere greeted him with chants of "We want God!" The pope never directly condemned the communist government. But he made it clear that no nation which treated its citizens as mere means of production was compatible with the Gospel. And he promised the Poles he would "cry with a loud voice" on behalf of Christians throughout all the "oft-forgotten nations" of Eastern Europe.[22]

It's no coincidence that within months of the exhilarating "nine days of freedom," as Poles called the pope's visit, a nationwide strike erupted. The immediate cause was the latest in a long series of price hikes and wage cuts announced by inept communist leaders.

The resoluteness with which striking workers insisted for the right to form independent labor unions was undoubtedly inspired by the pope's message during his visit. Everywhere, in train yards and docks, factories and schools, hospitals and newspaper offices, strikers erected crucifixes and banners of John Paul, prayed together, and dedicated their struggle to God. When John Paul publicly blessed them and said that their leader, the burly and mustachioed Lech Wałésa, was sent by God, it was the beginning of the end for communist rule in Poland.

It would take a few more years of battling governmental resistance before free elections took place in Poland. But John Paul's championship of the Church of Silence was the tipping point that roused Poland, helped to inspire the nonviolent revolutions that swept through the Soviet satellites in 1989, and ultimately led to the end of the USSR. The triumph seemed a clear vindication of the pope's insistence at Puebla that Christ, acting in and through his Church, was the only liberator needed.

Redemptive Suffering

"If you join your suffering to the suffering of Christ, you
will be privileged cooperators in the salvation of souls."[23]
—John Paul II, "Message to the Sick," February 11, 2005

On May 13, 1981, the unthinkable happened: An attempt was
made on the life of the pope. A Turkish hit man named Mehmet Ali
Agca fired several shots at John Paul as he greeted pilgrims in St.
Peter's Square. One bullet struck the pope's abdomen. By the time
he got to hospital, his blood pressure and pulse were so low that
he was given last rites. In surgery for six hours, it took John Paul
months to recuperate.

Although never proven, it's likely that the pope's would-be assas-
sin was hired by the Bulgarian government and the Soviet KGB.
John Paul's very public challenge to Poland's communist authorities
had crossed the line. Ridding the world of this troublesome priest
seemed the perfect solution.

During his recovery and afterward, John Paul was struck by the
fact that the assassination attempt fell on the anniversary of the first
of three 1917 appearances of the Virgin Mary at Fátima, Portugal.

Throughout his life, the pope was deeply devoted to Mary. Shortly after his mother's death, young Karol had turned to the Mother of God for comfort. At fifteen, he was president of the Marian Sodality in Wadowice.

While working in the quarry during the Nazi occupation he read and reread Louis de Montfort's classic *True Devotion to Mary* so many times that it nearly fell apart. At each important turning point in his ordained life, he prayed for her guidance. As pope, he adopted as his motto a vow of dedication to Mary, *Totus tuus* ("totally yours"), and made a point of praying before her shrines in every country he visited. Thirteen of his fourteen encyclicals evoke and recommend her. And as he was being rushed to the hospital after the 1981 shooting, he murmured, "Mary, my mother! Mary, my mother!"

For the rest of his days, John Paul was convinced that his life had been spared through Mary's intercession. "One hand fired, and another hand guided the bullet."[24] A year after the ordeal, he traveled to Fátima to place the bullet that nearly killed him in the crown of the shrine's statue of the Virgin Mary. Later, he gave the sash he had worn when he was shot, still spattered with his blood, to the shrine of the Black Madonna in Czestochowa, Poland. He also visited his assailant in prison and forgave him, an act that apparently both bewildered and touched Ali Agca.

In 1987, a year John Paul dedicated to the Blessed Mother, the pope released an encyclical, *Redemptoris Mater*, which he said he had long pondered in his heart. In it, he argued that "motherhood always establishes a unique and unrepeatable relationship"[25] between parent and child. When the crucified Jesus entrusted Mary and John the beloved disciple to each other, the Virgin became the mother of all humans. The special connection we have with her means both that she intercedes for us with a mother's tenderness, and that her universal motherhood makes all humans brothers and sisters.

John Paul's conviction that the Holy Mother saved him during the attempt on his life clearly strengthened his devotion to Mary. It also prompted him to write one of the most profound apostolic letters of his pontificate, *Salvifici Doloris* (Redemptive Suffering), in which he tried to make sense of his and the world's pain.

John Paul begins by acknowledging that everyone suffers, and suffering is an evil because it diminishes physical and psychological well-being. It can also be spiritually destructive, leading as it does to doubt the existence of God. Why would a good and loving God allow pain in his world? It's a question as old as Job.

The pope's answer is elegantly simple. As members of the mystical body, all Christians are grafted into Christ. We share, as it were, his spiritual DNA, enjoying an indissoluble link with him shared by our brothers and sisters. We know, by faith, that Christ's suffering was redemptive. Consequently, because we're joined to him and to all humankind, our suffering must somehow participate in his act of redemption as well.

In our suffering, we collaborate with Christ for the salvation of the world. Our suffering, in union with the cross of Christ, is therefore anything but random and meaningless. It is cosmically restorative, even though it may be a horrible burden to the sufferer. John Paul didn't intend to whitewash suffering. Doing so would have been both insensitive and false. But he did want to show that God can use even suffering for the betterment of humankind. It, like everything else, has a place in the economy of salvation.

To John Paul's mind, the suffering he endured at the hands of Ali Agca contributed to the redemptive collapse of communism. Because one of the Fátima Virgin's predictions had foretold the reconversion of Russia, he saw the date of the assassination attempt as a clear sign that his wound somehow contributed to the prophecy's fulfillment. When the pope visited Fátima for a second time on the tenth anniversary of the shooting—the same year that the Soviet Union broke apart—he knelt to thank the Virgin "for the unexpected changes that restored confidence to nations that had long been oppressed and humiliated."[26]

But during the same visit, he also sounded an alarm about the dangerous direction he saw the post-communist world headed. With Soviet oppression a thing of the past, John Paul II would dedicate himself to stemming the tide of "a vast theoretical and practical atheistic movement that appears to seek a new materialistic civilization."[27] Communism was no longer the threat. Now, unbridled and unashamed secularism, bolstered by runaway capitalism, was.

chapter six

At Odds with the World

"It is necessary to prepare immunizing defenses against certain viruses such as secularism, indifferentism, hedonistic consumerism, practical materialism, and the formal atheism that is so widely diffused today."[28]

—John Paul II, Letter to Juliusz Kydryski

In the decade that followed the collapse of the Soviet Union and the spread of democracy in Eastern Europe, the pope became convinced that the world faced an even greater, more seductive, enemy than political totalitarianism: the "viruses," as he called them, of secularism, consumerism, and materialism. In 1990, he rejoiced that communism, an ideology that "neglected and negated man['s] irrepressible longing for freedom and truth,"[29] was crumbling But only one year later, shocked by the rise of "thoughtless" self-indulgence in newly capitalist Poland, he issued an angry warning to his countrymen: "You mustn't confuse freedom with immorality."[30]

The problem with the capitalist dream of unlimited wealth is that it induced spiritual amnesia. The consumerist virus mutated worship of God into worship of goods and transformed God's earth into mere raw material to be exploited for profit. It encouraged humans to see one another as adversarial competitors for limited resources. It ignored the scriptural commands to care for the poor, the oppressed, and the weak, moral imperatives that even godless Marxism had recognized. And it made a mockery of morality by insisting that right and wrong are nothing more than matters of personal opinion based on appetite and aversion.

But moral truth, John Paul insisted, is not a fanciful creation of the will. Freedom collapses into license if the ethical principles it embraces aren't true. To refute "the whole civilization of desire and pleasure which is now lording over us,"[31] he wrote his two best and most controversial encyclicals. The first, released in 1993, was *Veritatis Splendor* (The Splendor of Truth). The second, published two years later, was *Evangelium Vitae* (The Gospel of Life). John Paul had touched upon the moral, social, and spiritual dangers of materialism in most of his earlier encyclicals. Now he tackled the problem with concentrated vigor.

Veritatis Splendor, which the pope worked on for some six years, explicitly addressed the world's "crisis of truth" that obscures the "moral sense" and risks making it "impossible to build up and to preserve the moral order."[32] One of the fundamental causes of this lamentable situation is the secular tendency to take freedom itself as the supreme value. But this leads to the chaos of rejecting any moral boundaries.

In contrast to this moral nihilism, John Paul argued that freedom is valuable only to the extent that it conforms to objective truth, embodied in the Christ who perpetually exemplifies "a love which gives itself completely to the brethren out of love for God."[33] Free submission to this law of love, not the unbridled pursuit of self-interest, is what "leads the human person to his own true good." Conscience, although essential, requires guidance by Church tradition and doctrine. "The Church seeks, with great love, to help all the faithful to form a moral conscience which will make judgments and lead to decisions in accordance with the truth."[34]

In *Veritatis Splendor,* John Paul defended the universality and permanence of the Church's moral doctrine. In *Evangelium Vitae,* he focused on the "culture of death" the rejection of objective values creates. A world in which the uninhibited pursuit of self-interest trumps everything else is indifferent at best to the sanctity of life. Sooner or later, the pope argued, it engages in a "war of the powerful against the weak," and the weakest members of society are unborn children and the chronically ill or elderly.

Disregard for life at its beginning and its end insidiously erodes concern for life across the board, leading to a "progressive weakening in individual consciences and society of the sense of the absolute and grave moral illicitness of the direct taking of all innocent human life."[35] Nor will appeals to civil laws that legalize abortion, euthanasia, or other kinds of killing such as capital punishment do. Civil law is legitimate only when it conforms to moral law, and moral law never condones statutes that encourage cultures of death.

Although the two encyclicals were widely hailed as courageous defenses of Church teaching, they were not without critics. Swiss theologian Hans Küng was one of the most vociferous, charging that John Paul had arrogantly conflated his own personal moral views with the Church's. At least one American bishop worried that the abstract moral theology defended in *Veritatis Splendor* offered no practical advice on how to behave morally. And *Evangelium Vitae* reignited some of the fury that *Humanae Vitae* had evoked in 1968.

John Paul was surprised by the sometimes ferocious push back his two encyclicals generated, and became even more certain that he needed to take a firm stand in defending doctrine and opposing the worldly viruses he now suspected had begun to infect the Church as well. In his campaign against the culture of death's divorce of freedom and truth, he sometimes came across as too authoritarian.

Critics accused him of being unwilling to consider alternative perspectives on hot-button issues such as abortion; too ready to censure dissident theologians such as Leonardo Boff, Charles Curran, and

Hans Küng; and too unbending when it came to priestly celibacy and the ordination of women. They conceded that as the vicar of Christ, John Paul was called to protect the faith from both external and internal threats. They just disagreed with him about what was and wasn't a threat. The pope, for his part, insisted that in matters of salvation, the faithful were obliged by their baptismal vows to honor the doctrines handed down from one generation to the next and most recently reconfirmed by Vatican II.

chapter seven

Blessed Are the Peacemakers

"Do we not believe in Jesus Christ, the Prince of Peace?"[36]
—John Paul II, *Ut Unum Sint*

If liberals were angered by John Paul's repudiation of moral relativism, many traditionalists and conservatives were equally unhappy with his firm condemnation of war, his efforts at ecumenical reconciliation and interfaith dialogue, and his public apologies for past sins of the Church.

John Paul's aversion to the violence was born from the horror of World War II and the experience afterward of living under the jackboot of Stalinism. His birth town of Wadowice is only a few kilometers from Owicim, better known to the world as Auschwitz. Nearly all of Wadowice's two thousand Jews, some of whom Lolek Wojtyła knew and played with, perished there.

Haunted by their murders, he went on pilgrimage to Auschwitz many times as priest, bishop, and pontiff. The scale of suffering inflicted by the war and the repressive climate of fear in postwar communist Poland convinced him that Jesus's teachings about nonviolence had to be heeded.

As a Catholic, he accepted the doctrine of just war endorsed by the Church since the fifth century. But he knew that there were nearly no circumstances in which going to war could be morally justified. "War," he said, "is never just another means that one can choose to employ for settling differences between nations."[37] Given its horrific costs, it should always be the absolute last resort after all other options have been genuinely exhausted. War "destroys the lives of innocent people, teaches how to kill, throws into upheaval even the lives of those who do the killing, and leaves behind a trail of resentment and hatred."[38]

From the very start of his pontificate, John Paul attempted to forestall or mitigate armed conflict between the world's nations. In late 1978, he tried to defuse a quarrel between Chile and Argentina over the Beagle Channel Islands. When the Falklands War erupted three years later, he made a special visit to Buenos Aires in the hope of stopping the killing.

One of the reasons he rejected liberation theology was his association of it with of armed revolt, and throughout Poland's struggle against Soviet domination he stressed nonviolent resistance. He denounced the 1991 Gulf War as an avoidable "darkness," and twelve years later pled with George W. Bush to refrain from using 9/11 as a pretext for declaring war against Iraq. Throughout the end of the Cold War era and afterward, he consistently urged the superpowers to eliminate or at least reduce their nuclear arsenals.

Although he condemned war, John Paul recognized that it was often sparked by real grievances such as "injustices suffered, legitimate aspirations frustrated, poverty and exploitation."[39] To redress these ills, world leaders needed to recognize the economic and spiritual interdependence of the world's people. Humans are bound together economically by the globalization of markets and spiritually by "the common fatherhood of God."[40]

In the light of these indissoluble bonds, a new model of world citizenship based on unity or "solidarity" should replace the current international distrust and competition which leaves two-thirds of the world's population in poverty. For John Paul, solidarity was a preeminent Christian virtue, the social correlate of the spiritual interconnectedness of the Body of Christ, and the necessary condition for peace.

The pope recognized that religious disagreements are major causes of violence, and he resolved to do everything in his power to bring about some measure of solidarity between Catholic, Protestant, and Orthodox Christians on the one hand and Christians and non-Christians on the other. As he announced in the 1991 encyclical *Centesimus Annus,* all faith traditions are called to "offer the unanimous witness of our common convictions regarding the dignity of man."[41] Four years later, he devoted an entire encyclical, *Ut Unum Sint*, That They All May Be One, to the Church's commitment to healing the ruptures in the worldwide Christian family.

Throughout his pontificate, John Paul sought with mixed success to establish closer relationships between Catholics and the Anglican and Orthodox churches. He was more successful in his efforts to reach an agreement with the Lutheran World Federation over the meaning of justification by faith, one of the points of theological dispute that led to the Reformation.

In 1986 and again in 1991, John Paul convened world conferences on religion and peace attended by representatives of the world's different faith traditions. He made overtures to Muslim leaders on several occasions, met regularly with Jewish leaders, and in 1986 became the first pontiff to visit a Jewish temple when he worshiped with the chief rabbi of Italy in Rome's Great Synagogue. During the service, he referred to the Jewish people as the elder brothers and sisters of Christians, and in 2000, while praying at Jerusalem's Wailing Wall, an infirm John Paul asked forgiveness for the Church's past sins against the Jewish people.

It was a mark of the humility that Karol Wojtyła brought to the papacy—and this despite criticisms that he ruled with an authoritarianism that ill fit the collegial model endorsed by Vatican II—that he felt the need, as head of the Roman Catholic Church, to apologize for the wounds Catholics had inflicted on others through the centuries. His apology to the Jews for past persecutions was just one of his acts of repentance. On behalf of Catholics, the pope also begged forgiveness for violence against Protestants in Europe's religious wars, for injustices against women and ethnic groups, for not doing more to prevent the slave trade or the Holocaust, for complicity in the genocide of Mesoamericans, and for the persecution and silencing of Galileo.

Starting in 2001, an aged John Paul expressed contrition on several occasions, again on behalf of the Church, for the sexual abuse perpetrated by priests against children and adults. Critics dismissed his apology, with some justification, as doing too little and coming too late. But what's not contestable is the genuine sorrow and pain that lay behind it.

Duc in altum!

> "At the beginning of the new millennium...and [as] a new stage of the Church's journey begins, our hearts ring out with the words of Jesus when one day, after speaking to the crowds from Simon's boat, he invited the apostles to 'put out into the deep' for a catch: *Duc in altum*.... These words ring out for us today."[42]
>
> —John Paul II, *Novo Millennio Ineunte*

If the Church is to be a sign of contradiction and hope to an increasingly secular world, she must remain fervent in her fidelity to the Good News of Jesus Christ. By the second decade of his pontificate, John Paul was worried that the salt was losing its savor.

Many Catholics throughout the world were ignoring Church teachings about sexuality, prominent Catholic theologians were publicly disputing established doctrine, and his beloved Poland, once so strong in the faith, seemed more focused on the pursuit of wealth and pleasure than on God. His fear that the Church was in danger of forgetting its identity goes a long way toward explaining the authoritarian streak in John Paul's later years. As pope, he felt keenly his responsibility to hold things together.

By 1990, John Paul concluded that one way to revitalize the Church was to remind its members that they were charged by Jesus to "go and make disciples of all nations." For most of the Church's history, its missionary activities had been directed outwards to those who hadn't yet heard the Good News. But in his eighth encyclical, *Redemptoris Missio*, John Paul shifted the focus to internal evangelization. What he had in mind were those "countries with ancient Christian roots and occasionally in the younger Churches as well, where entire groups of the baptized have lost a sense of the faith, or even no longer consider themselves members of the Church, and live a life far removed from Christ and his Gospel."[43]

In these areas, which included vast regions of Europe, North America, and Australia, "what is needed is a 'new evangelization' or a 're-evangelization.'" The New Evangelization's aim was to reawake Christians who no longer saw the relevance or felt the draw of their own tradition so that they could resist and transform the culture of death.

To further the New Evangelization, John Paul dedicated himself to visiting and uplifting Catholics in as many countries as he could. Throughout his nearly twenty-seven-year pontificate, he made over one hundred pastoral trips outside of Italy, visiting each of the six inhabited continents and traveling over a million kilometers—equal to about three times the distance between earth and moon. He was certainly the most-traveled pope, and probably one of the most-traveled humans, in history. During these visits, depending on his destination, he inspired, comforted, exhorted, or admonished, always with the aim of strengthening local churches and revitalizing faith.

John Paul also recognized that the future of the Church lay in the hands of the next generation, and early on devoted himself to properly evangelizing young people. He found it a joyful ministry; from his earliest days as a priest he had relished working with youth. He launched the campaign with his 1985 apostolic letter *Dilecti Amici,* in which, after telling young people that their youth isn't merely their own property but belongs to the whole Church, he impressed on them their great responsibility to the faith. "On you depends the future, on you depends also the end of this millennium and the beginning of the next. So do not be passive."[44] The following year, the pope convened the first World Youth Day, an international gathering of Catholic youth, held every two or three years at different spots around the world, in which "the young people of the world could meet Christ, who is eternally young, and could learn from him how to be *bearers of the Gospel to other young people.*"[45]

The pope knew that reevangelization needed to reawaken passion in souls grown tepid but also speak to intellects that, immersed in a secular ethos, had doubts about faith's credibility. His world travels, youth ministry, and thousands of sermons spoke in large part to the heart. In his 1998 encyclical *Fides et Ratio,* he spoke to the head by rigorously scrutinizing the relationship between faith and reason. His aim was to show that the two complement rather than compete with one another: Faith without reason mutates into superstition, and reason without faith leads to nihilism.

Together, the two strengthen and embolden each other. "Faith asks that its object be understood with the help of reason; and at the summit of its searching, reason acknowledges that it cannot do without what faith presents."[46] John Paul's point was that the faith is neither absurd nor intellectually lightweight. The Gospel may be scandalous in the eyes of its cultured despisers, but it is hardly irrational.

From the very beginning of his pontificate, John Paul looked forward to the Holy Year that would mark the start of Christianity's third millennium. His failing health in his final decade led some observers to wonder if he would make it. But the pope's confidence never waned. He believed that the Virgin Mary had deflected Ali Agca's bullet so that he could lead the Church into a new millennium of evangelization.

For over two decades, the pope had been repeating what the angel Gabriel told Mary: Do not be afraid! Trust in God! Risk everything for God's promise! He returned to the same theme in his apostolic letter *Novo Millennio Ineunte*, At the Beginning of the New Millennium, released in January 2001. Citing the story in Luke's Gospel in which Jesus invites Peter and the apostles to "put out into the deep" if they want to catch fish, he recommended the same radical trust when it came to evangelizing the third millennium. *Duc in altum!* he urged the faithful. Throw yourself trustingly into God's depths! "Remember the past with gratitude, live the present with enthusiasm, and look forward to the future with confidence."[47] Cultivate personal holiness through prayer and then fearlessly proclaim the Good News, recalling those who have fallen away and amazing those who have not yet heard it.

John Paul's *Novo Millennio Ineunte*, although soberly reminding Christians of the challenges facing them, was hopeful and even jubilant. But it was also a kind of personal *nunc dimittis*. The pope knew that his body was failing him, and that it would soon be time to pass the torch to others.

chapter nine

Preaching from the Cross

"I offer my sufferings so that God's plan may be completed and his Word spread among the peoples."[48]

—John Paul II, 2005 Lenten Message

As pope, John Paul wrote the letters AMDG in the top left corner of every piece of paper he signed. They stood for *Ad majorem Dei gloriam*, "For the greater glory of God," and testified to the pontiff's intention to dedicate his every thought, word, and deed to the Lord. At the end of his life, when he had nothing more to give, he offered up his dying as a final oblation to God and a gift for Christians around the world.

John Paul's resolution to do everything, even dying, for the greater glory of God was sustained by an intense prayer life. Images of the pope at prayer have become iconic. The bowed head, tightly shut eyes, and clenched fingers around the shaft of his papal crozier testify to the depth of his concentration when communing with God. The contemplative impulse that made him yearn to become a cloistered Carmelite in his younger years remained with him to the end. As pontiff, John Paul became a man of action. But he was first and foremost a man of prayer.

Physically vigorous as a boy, youth, and man, Karol Wojtyła glowed with rugged health when he was elected pope. The world was enthralled by photographs of the athletic pope skiing in the Dolomites. But the medical aftereffects of the 1981 assassination attempt as well as the killing pace of his work as pontiff eventually began to weaken John Paul's robust constitution.

By 1991, the first signs of Parkinson's disease appeared. The following summer, he endured major surgery to remove a benign tumor from his colon. The next year he fell twice in his Vatican apartment, the second time breaking a hip. The year after that, he was back in the hospital for an appendectomy. All the while, the Parkinson's incrementally eroded the coordination of his muscles. By the end of his pontificate, he could barely walk, his speech was slurred, his head was permanently tilted as if he couldn't sustain its weight, and his mouth drooled. It was heartbreaking to witness the steady deterioration of a man who once had been so vibrantly full of life.

And witness it the world did, because from the beginning John Paul refused to keep his infirmities secret. For years, the secrecy surrounding a pope's health had meant, as Vatican watchers joked, that no pope was sick until his death was announced. But in keeping with the theology of his *Salvifici Doloris,* John Paul believed that his physical decline, participating as it did in the suffering of Christ, also mysteriously participated in its redemptive power. He wanted a suffering world to know that pain and agony were not meaningless, that even mortal sickness, if understood for what it is, is not only endurable but actually an opportunity for service.

As he wrote in *Memory and Identity,* his final book, "The passion of Christ on the Cross gave a radically new meaning to suffering, transforming it from within.... It is this suffering which burns and consumes evil with the flame of love."[49] So John Paul made his own physical suffering public, displaying his misery for all to see, not to garner pity but in the hope that his manner of dying would inspire others to better cope with their own suffering. Sustained by prayer to the end, he showed the world how to die without being defeated by death. He wanted everyone to see that illness and dying "are not...any less fruitful in God's plan" than health and well-being.[50] Even the way in which one died could be done for the greater glory of God.

John Paul's last trip abroad was in August 2004, less than a year before his death. Despite his infirmities, he made a pilgrimage to Lourdes, the site in France where the Virgin Mary appeared to Bernadette Soubirous in 1858. The occasion was the one-hundred-fiftieth anniversary of Pope Pius IX's promulgation of the Immaculate Conception of Mary, the dogma that the Virgin Mother was born free of the taint of original sin. But significantly, given the state of John Paul's health, Lourdes is also the Christian world's most famous healing shrine, visited each year by around six million pilgrim-invalids who come to drink the grotto's waters and pray for a miraculous cure.

John Paul didn't go to Lourdes with similar hopes. He had already dedicated his loosening grip on life to God, and would see it through to the end without expectation or desire of a reprieve. He went to show his solidarity with the millions of people at Lourdes and around the globe who endured the ravages of illness and disease, and to uphold them in their ordeal. He also went to remind the world one last time that the sick should be lovingly cared for rather than shunted out of sight in impersonal medical facilities, much less denied medical treatment for financial reasons. As he had written in 1992 when he proclaimed the first annual World Day of the Sick, "Love for the suffering is the sign and measure of the degree of civilization and progress of a people."[51]

After his visit to Lourdes, John Paul's health continued its downward course. A bout of flu in February 2005 was the beginning of the end for the weakened pope. It brought him such respiratory distress that an emergency tracheotomy was performed to keep him from suffocating. The procedure left John Paul with a nearly inaudible voice. From then on, the pope's final message to the world was preached silently from the cross. He held on for a bit longer before collapsing while at prayer in his private chapel on March 31. Two days later, he returned to God. At the end, his thoughts were with his two great loves: God and his homeland. His final words, murmured in Polish, were "Let me go to the Lord."[52]

Conclusion: Legacy

"The first age is at a close,
the second begins.
We take in our hands the outline of the inevitable time."[53]
—Karol Wojtyła, "Stanislas"

In death as in life, John Paul II was a controversial figure. Even many of his admirers admitted that he seemed at times a man of contradictions: a devotee of Mary but an opponent of women's ordination, a staunch defender of human rights but a harsh critic of liberation theology, and a man who regularly invoked the documents of Vatican II but whose leadership style minimized the council's call for collegiality.

Yet the contradictoriness attributed to John Paul is actually more often than not a consequence of his refusal to be fitted with either a liberal or conservative label—a continuous source of frustration for those who wanted to neatly pigeonhole him—instead going where he believed the Spirit led him, even when the destination surprised and sometimes disappointed people. He was not, of course, a perfect man, and occasionally real tensions flawed his thinking and judgment. But there was more continuity than inconsistency in John Paul's life. What critics saw as contradiction was usually complexity.

What abides is the fact that John Paul II was one of the greatest popes ever to steer the barque of Peter and one of the greatest men of his generation. What's also unquestionable is the intense devotion to God and the loving concern for human well-being that he displayed throughout his entire life. His work, prayers, and suffering—and, it might be argued, even the firm hand that he brought to the papacy—changed the political landscape of the twentieth century and revitalized the Church. Pope Benedict XVI, in announcing the beatification of John Paul in 2011, accurately captured his legacy.

> He rightly reclaimed for Christianity that impulse of hope which had in some sense faltered before Marxism and the ideology of progress. He restored to Christianity its true face as a religion of hope, to be lived in history in an "Advent" spirit, in a personal and communitarian existence directed to Christ, the fullness of humanity and the fulfillment of all our longings for justice and peace.[54]

John Paul's canonization two and a half years later by Pope Francis was a joyous and grateful affirmation of this legacy.

Notes

1. John Paul II, *Gift and Mystery* (New York: Doubleday, 1996), 88.

2. Quoted in "How to Live Holiness According to John Paul II," Rome Reports TV News Agency. http://www.youtube.com/watch?v=OcbJ_GJDbNg.

3. John Paul II, *Rise, Let Us be on Our Way,* trans. Walter Ziemba (New York: Warner, 2004), 191.

4. Quoted in Carl Bernstein & Marco Politi, *His Holiness* (New York: Doubleday, 1996), 25.

5. Karol Wojtyła, "Over this your white grave," in *Collected Poems,* trans. Jerzy Peterkiewicz (New York: Random House, 1986), 2.

6. John Paul II, *Gift and Mystery,* 6

7. Quoted in Meg Greene, *Pope John Paul II* (Westport, Conn.: Greenwood, 2003), 39.

8. Quoted in Jonathan Kwitney, *Man of the Century: The Life and Times of John Paul II* (New York: Henry Holt, 1997), 56.

9. Quoted in Bernstein and Politi, 57.

10. Quoted in George Weigel, *Witness to Hope* (New York: Harper, 2001), 68.

11. John Paul II, *Gift and Mystery,* 44–45.

12. Quoted in Kwitney, 80.

13 John Paul II, "Master in the Faith," Apostolic Letter, December 1990.

14. John Paul II, *Gift and Mystery*, 71.

15. John Paul II, *Gift and Mystery*, 73.

16. Cardinal Karol Wojtyła, Pastoral Letter, May 8, 1977.

17. Karol Wojtyła, "Synodus," in *Collected Poems,* 104.

18. Quoted in Bernstein and Politi, 128.

19. John Paul II, Inaugural Mass Homily, October 22, 1978, 5.

20. Address to the Third General Council of the Latin American Episcopate (Puebla, Mexico), January 28, 1979, III.2.

21. Meeting with Mexican Indios (Cuilapan, Mexico), January 29, 1979.

22. Quoted in Bernstein and Politi, 218.

23. John Paul II, *Silence Transformed into Life: The Testament of His Final Year* (Hyde Park, N.Y.: New City Press, 2006), 120.

24. Quoted in Weigel, 413.

25. *Redemptoris Mater,* 45.

26. Quoted in Tad Szulc, *Pope John Paul II* (New York: Scribner, 1995), 366.

27. John Paul II, Remarks at Fatima, Portugal. Quoted in Alan Riding, "Pope visisits Fatima to offer thanks," *New York Times,* May 14, 1991.

28. Quoted in Bernstein and Politi, 496.

29. Bernstein and Politi, 483.

30. Bernstein and Politi, 487.

31. Bernstein and Politi, 492.

32. *Veritatis Splendor,* 93.

33. *Veritatis Splendor,* 20.

34. *Veritatis Splendor,* 85.

35. *Evangelium Vitae,* 57.

36. *Ut Unum Sint,* 76.

37. John Paul II, Address to the Diplomatic Corps, 13 January 2003.

38. *Centesimus Annus,* 52.

39. *Centesimus Annus,* 52.

40. *Sollicitudo Rei Socialis,* 40.

41. *Centesimus Annus,* 60.

42. *Novo Millennio Ineunte.* Apostolic Letter, January 6, 2001.

43. *Redemptoris Missio,* 33.

44. *Dilecti Amici,* Apostolic Letter, March 31, 1985.

45. John Paul II, Evening Vigil Address, World Youth Day, Toronto, July 27, 2002.

46. *Fides et Ratio,* 42.

47. *Novo Millennio Ineunte,* 1.

48. John Paul II, *Silence Transformed into Life,* 115.

49. John Paul II, *Memory and Identity* (New York: Rizzoli, 2005), 186.

50. John Paul II, *Silence Transformed into Life,* 111.

51. John Paul II, "Message for the First Annual World Day of the Sick," October 21, 1992.

52. Stanislaw Dziwisz, *A Life with Karol: My Forty-Year Friendship with the Man Who Became Pope,* trans. Adrian Walker (New York: Doubleday, 2008), 257.

53. Karol Wojtyła, "Stanislas," in *Collected Poems,* 172.

54. Benedict XVI, Homily, Papal Mass on the Occasion of the Beatification of the Servant of God John Paul II, May 1, 2011.

Bibliography

Benedict XVI. Homily, Papal Mass on the Occasion of the Beatification of the Servant of God John Paul II, May 1, 2011.

Bernstein, Carl, and Marco Politi. *His Holiness: John Paul II and the Hidden History of Our Time* (New York: Doubleday, 1996).

Centesimus Annus.

Dilecti Amici, Apostolic Letter, March 31, 1985.

Dziwisz, Stanislaw. *A Life with Karol: My Forty-Year Friendship with the Man Who Became Pope,* trans. Adrian Walker (New York: Doubleday, 2008).

Evangelium Vitae.

Fides et Ratio.

Greene, Meg. *Pope John Paul II: A Biography* (Westport, Conn.: Greenwood, 2003).

John Paul II. *Gift and Mystery: On the Fiftieth Anniversary of My Priestly Ordination* (New York: Image, 1999).

———. *Memory and Identity: Conversations at the Dawn of a Millennium* (New York: Rizzoli, 2005).

———. *Rise, Let Us be on Our Way,* trans. Walter Ziemba (New York: Grand Central, 2004).

————. *Silence Transformed into Life: The Testament of His Final Year* (Hyde Park, N.Y.: New City, 2006).

Kwitney, Jonathan. *Man of the Century: The Life and Times of John Paul II* (New York: Henry Holt, 1997).

Novo Millennio Ineunte. Apostolic Letter, January 6, 2001.

Redemptoris Mater.

Redemptoris Missio.

Salvifici Doloris, Apostolic Letter, February 11, 1984.

Sollicitudo Rei Socialis.

Szulc, Tad. *Pope John Paul II* (New York: Scribner, 1995).

Ut Unum Sint.

Veritatis Splendor.

Weigel, George *Witness to Hope: The Biography of Pope John Paul II* (New York: Harper, 2001).

Wojtyła, Karol. *Collected Poems*, trans. Jerzy Peterkiewicz (New York: Random House, 1982).

ABOUT THE AUTHOR

Kerry Walters is a professor of philosophy and peace and justice studies at Gettysburg College in Pennsylvania. He is a prolific author whose recent books include *Giving Up god to Find God: Breaking Free of Idolatry*; *The Art of Dying and Living*; and *John XXIII: A Short Biography*.